Ednah Dow Littlehale Cheney

Patience

a series of games with cards

Ednah Dow Littlehale Cheney

Patience
a series of games with cards

ISBN/EAN: 9783744736749

Printed in Europe, USA, Canada, Australia, Japan

Cover: Foto ©Andreas Hilbeck / pixelio.de

More available books at **www.hansebooks.com**

PATIENCE:

A

SERIES OF GAMES WITH CARDS.

COMPILED BY

MRS. E. D. CHENEY.

"LET PATIENCE HAVE HER PERFECT WORK."

Second Edition, with Additio.

BOSTON:

LEE AND SHEPARD, PUBLISHERS.

NEW YORK:

LEE, SHEPARD AND DILLINGHAM.

1875.

STEREOTYPED AT THE
BOSTON STEREOTYPE FOUNDRY,
19 Spring Lane.

PREFACE.

THE Game, or rather style of game, called PATIENCE, — for it is not one, but manifold; — has long been a great favorite in Europe, but is familiar to our people only in one or two of its simplest forms, under the French name of *Soli taire.*

I have endeavored, in this little book, to naturalize it here, in all its charming variety. I believe it to be an innocent and agreeable amusement, well fitted to refresh the mind after severer labors, and to beguile the weary hours of invalidism or seclusion. Its great advantage consists in the fact that it is played by one person alone. Yet it can also become a social pleasure, by others looking on and sharing in the interest of the chase and the pleasure of success. The mother may be plying her busy needle, and yet share in the counsel and enjoyment of her child, who is planning out his game of Patience beside her. It does not produce the feverish excitement of games of chance and skill played against an opponent. The contest is against fate, or chance, or circumstance, as you choose to call it, alone, and there is no feeling of rivalry or opposition excited. In most of the games both skill and chance enter into the account, and some of them tax the ingenuity of the player very thoroughly; but in others only quick observation is needed. The mind is thus gently stimulated, while the quiet progress of the game tends to cultivate the important virtue whose name it bears. The invalid, too feeble to lay out the cards, will often be entertained by watching the progress of the game in another's hands.

The interest of Patience is sometimes enhanced by using it as a fortune-teller.

The player will wish for the success of some enterprise he has at heart, and will fancy that his good or ill fortune in getting out the game is an augury of his luck in more important matters. It may often prove so, for the quiet attention and calm patience which enable one to seize the best opportunities in the mimic struggle, may help to win success in the more important affairs of life.

Patience is a great favorite among all the people of the Germanic races in Europe. Miss Bremer frequently alludes to it in her charming pictures of life in Sweden. For instance, in "The Home," Louise calms her anxious thoughts by playing " Patience ; " and many others of her characters find it a good specific against weariness and trouble. It has been introduced both into France and England, and was, we are told, a solace to the weary hours of exile at St. Helena.

It remains for me to indicate the sources whence I have derived my information. The majority of these games are taken from a little book published first in France, and afterward translated into English, which accidentally came to my notice. So much of the awkwardness of a translation remained in the English book, that the descriptions of the games were often extremely obscure, and what may have been graceful sentiment in the original became absurd in the dilution. I have, therefore, entirely rewritten all the descriptions of the games, and tested them all by experiment, and have added diagrams wherever it seemed necessary to a perfect understanding. Several additional games, some of which are entirely different from any in the English book, have been gathered from other sources.

As many of the games require a large number of cards upon the table at once, it has been found convenient to use small-sized cards. It being difficult to procure these of good quality, the publishers have had some prepared to accompany this book.

Although I have long wished the publication of these games, for my own convenience and that of others, esteeming any increase of the means of innocent amusement a public good, yet my purpose was stimulated by the wish to procure funds for establishing libraries for the Freedmen's Schools at the South. All the compiler's percentage will be devoted to this object, and the very liberal allowance made by the publishers leads me to hope, that, while contributing to the entertainment of the home circle and the solace of the invalid's couch, I shall also have the pleas-

ure of sending instruction and encour-
agement to many a school at the South,
and so — " PATIENCE may have her perfect work."

EDNAH D. CHENEY.

FOREST HILL ST.,
    November 15, 1869.

PREFACE

TO THE SECOND EDITION.

—•◦•—

PATIENCE has met with so much favor, that I gladly take the opportunity of a new edition to make such corrections and additions as four years' use has suggested to me. These consist only of slight verbal additions to make the text more clear, and of three new games which have come to my notice, and which are very valuable. They are the only important additions that I have found, although many persons have kindly told me of games which they had played; but I have always found them to be only slight variations of some already in the book. As I am fully convinced of the great value of this amusement as a resource to invalids and rest to over-wearied brains, I should be glad to make it of permanent value and as complete as possible, and I shall be grateful for any suggestions of new games, whose principle varies from any of those I have already given.

CONTENTS.

		PAGE
SOLITAIRE,	One pack.	17
GRANDFATHERS,	Two packs.	20
THE SULTAN,	Two packs.	23
PATERNAL,	One pack.	27
THE TRIOS, A VARIATION OF PATERNAL,	One pack.	31
MUSICAL,	One pack.	33
THE LEGITIMIST,	Two packs.	36
FOURTEEN,	Two packs.	33
THE WINDMILL.	Two packs.	40
SALIQUE LAW,	Two packs.	44
PUSH PIN,	Two packs.	47
LITTLE LOTS.	Euchre pack.	49
WANDERING CARD,	One pack.	51
PATIENCE AT ST. HELENA,	Two packs.	54
BLOCKADE,	Two packs.	58
NUMBER ELEVEN,	One or two packs.	60
THE EGYPTIAN,	One pack.	62

15

THE CLOCK,	*One pack.*	66
DOUBLE JUMP,	*One pack.*	70
NIVERNAISE,	*Two packs.*	72
DUCHESS OF LUYNES,	*Two packs.*	74
PICTURE,	*Two packs.*	76
LADY OF THE MANOR,	*Two packs.*	78
HONORS,	*Two packs.*	83
PUZZLE,	*Euchre pack.*	86
KNAVE'S DIAL,	*One or two packs.*	88
BRUNETTE AND BLONDE,	*Two packs.*	90
THE SQUARE,	*Two packs.*	92
THE QUEEN'S PARTY,	*One pack.*	94
FIFTEEN IN A ROW,	*Two packs.*	96
NAPOLEON, OR THE PET GAME,	*Two packs.*	99
THE OLD STAGER,	*Two packs.*	102
CORNERS,	*One pack.*	104
RANK AND FILE,	*Two packs.*	108
THE TOAD,	*Two packs.*	111
EXPLANATION OF TERMS USED,		113

GAMES OF PATIENCE.

———•◦•———

SOLITAIRE.

ONE PACK.

THIS is the simplest form of Patience, and yet it requires no little skill to play it judiciously. It is well adapted to invalids who cannot bear much effort.

Shuffle the cards well. Lay the four aces as they come in a row. Place the other cards as they appear from the pack, on the aces in order, without following suit; as ace, deuce, three,

2

four, &c. ; this is called putting the cards in Families. Place the cards which do not fit on these in due order, in four piles below, and whenever the top card will go on the upper line in regular sequence, you can use it, which will thus free the card beneath it. The skill consists in deciding on which of these four piles to place the cards from the pack, and which card to use, if you have two top cards of the same number. Of course you must not, if you can help it, place a higher card on a lower ; but if you have already four piles, this will often be unavoidable ; you must then endeavor to get off the higher cards, to free those beneath. According to the old, strict rule, of not looking to see what cards are beneath the top card, it becomes an excellent exercise of memory, to recall in which pile are the cards you want at the moment. It is not well to place many cards of the same number in one pile. If you can complete the families in the upper row to the kings, you have succeeded in your first trial of patience; if not, you have failed.

You may make this game still easier, by taking out the aces, and placing them in the upper row, before beginning the game; or you may make it more difficult by following suit in the families, in which case you are entitled to take up the lower piles, re-shuffle them, and re-lay them twice.

GRANDFATHERS.

TWO PACKS.

THE origin of this name is not known. It differs materially from Solitaire, as in this game one set of families proceeds upward, from ace to king, the other downward, from king to ace. Having shuffled both packs together, as usual, lay off two rows, of ten cards each, on the table. As the aces and kings appear, place them in two rows. You can use any of the cards you have laid down, in forming your families, but you must arrange them according to suits; that is, you must put all hearts upon the king or ace of hearts, and do the same with spades, clubs, and diamonds. When your first two rows are full, you may cover each card with another, placing it at your pleasure. In this consists the skill of the game; for, as you can only use the top card, it is important to leave uncovered such cards as you are likely soon to want. Should you have covered all your cards before using up the pack, and not be able to place any of them on your families, you can lay off three more from the pack; and should this not enable you to succeed, you have the privilege of drawing one.

If you have played all the cards without completing your families, you can draw any card from the table and put

it on the piles, which may enable you
to go on farther. Should you still
be unsuccessful, the Grandfathers have
proved too difficult for you this time,
and you must try again.

THE SULTAN.

TWO PACKS.

THIS is, perhaps, the most curious and interesting of all the games of Patience, and if successful, it forms a pretty picture of the Sultan or King of Hearts surrounded by his eight Queens. As it is rather difficult to understand the arrangement, we have prepared a little diagram to illustrate it.

Take out the ace of hearts and all the kings. Place one king of hearts in the centre. Just above him place the ace of hearts, and below him the other king of hearts. On each side of the ace place the kings of clubs, who represent war. On each side of the first king of hearts are the kings of diamonds, representing the treasury; and on the lower line, each side of the second king of hearts, are the kings of spades, representing the industrial forces. Then shuffle the remaining cards, and lay off from the pack. Put the first four cards on one side of the square formed by the kings, placing the ends of the cards towards the square. Put the next four cards on the other side in a similar manner: these eight cards form the Divan. Leaving the Sultan untouched, form the other families, by placing the aces on the kings, and so piling, in regular succession, according to suits, end-

ing with the queens. Place all cards
which you cannot immediately use in a
pile on the table, which is called the
Stock. You can use the card you are
laying off from the pack or the top
card of the stock, or any card in the
divan, in forming your families. When
a card is taken from the divan, you
may fill its place either by the top card
from the stock, or by the next card from
the pack, as you think most likely to
be favorable to your purpose.

When you have exhausted the pack,
you can take up the stock and use it as
a pack, always keeping your divan full.
This you can do twice. Some skill is
required in placing the cards in the
divan, and in selecting them for use,
and constant care is needed that no

opportunity of placing a card in the families escapes you. You will, after a little experience, generally be rewarded with success.

PATERNAL.

ONE PACK.

THIS game, which is very interesting from its varied complications, was named Paternal because of the pleasure it afforded to an old gentleman who was accustomed to play it a great deal in the long winter evenings. We wish he could have had the added pleasure of the variety of amusing games which we have the pleasure of presenting to our readers.

In this game we have, for the first time, the feature of Marriages; that is, the privilege of placing a top or end card on another of the same suit, which is either next above or next below it in number.

Lay the four aces in a row; lay out all the other cards in piles of three, spreading them a little, so that you can see those beneath. You can use only the top card; but you can form marriages to any extent, thus enabling you often to free the top card, and to get out the whole suit. The families are piled upwards upon the aces, following suit. The skill consists in forming the marriages so as not to cover other cards, which you may presently want to use in your families. If you do not succeed in completing your families from the first piles of cards, you take up your piles, shuffle them, and lay them

down agáin in the same way, going
through the process of forming marriages. You may repeat this a third
time if necessary. You have also the
privilege of drawing one card, but you
should be careful not to use this privilege the first or second time, unless
you see clearly that by so doing you
can win the game; for if you have but
three cards left in the last trial, they
may lie upon one another, so that you
cannot use them. This game requires
a good large table, and several persons
can assist with advice and sympathy, so
as to make it quite a social game.

There are many modifications of this
game. Some persons only make the
marriages by putting lower cards on
higher. Others do not allow any relay-

ing of the cards, or drawing, but instead of these privileges, when a king is the top card of a trio, you may take it off and lay it upon the table, and place lower cards upon it in succession, thus giving you an additional chance.

THE TRIOS.

A VARIATION OF "PATERNAL."

ONE PACK.

LAY off the cards in threes as in the former game, but divide the last four cards into twos. The families are to be formed on the four aces following suit. Only the top cards of the piles can be used. You can form marriages by placing a lower card on one next higher, without regard to suit, but you cannot put a higher card on a lower, nor have more than three on one

pile at any time. You can also put a
king on a king, a queen on a queen, and
a knave on a knave. You have no privilege of relaying the piles or drawing a
card.

MUSICAL.

ONE PACK.

THIS game is so named because it is a very ingenious arrangement of numbers in two scales. It is entirely unlike any other game in the book. It requires very little skill, as it depends almost entirely on the accidental arrangement of the cards by shuffling, and it is not often successful; but even if you fail, you will enjoy the ingenuity of the arrangement. Place eight cards in two horizontal lines, putting the ace, deuce, three, and four of any suit in the first line, and a two, four, six, eight, in the second, thus: —

$$1 - 2 - 3 - 4$$
$$2 - 4 - 6 - 8$$

Then play from the pack, putting on the lower line any card whose pits make the sum of those of the card on the upper line and the one below it. For instance, if you turn up a nine, you can place it below the three, as six and three are nine; if a six, put it below the two, since four and two are six. Then you will have a place for an eight under the two, for six and two are eight, &c. Knaves count eleven, queens twelve, kings thirteen. If the number amounts to more than thirteen, you take the amount beyond as the denomination for the lower card. Thus, knave and three would be ace, queen and four would be three, and so on. All cards which cannot be immediately used, are placed in a stock, of which you can use the top card as opportunity offers. You can turn the stock twice. If successful, the lower line will be all kings.

THE LEGITIMIST.

TWO PACKS.

THIS name is of French origin, but it seems to have no special adaptation to the game. It may have been applied to it from some old royalist, who solaced his years of exile with the company of mimic kings and queens. It requires close attention, but is not otherwise difficult.

Take a king and place it at the left. Then, having shuffled your cards well together, begin to lay them off. You place in succession, in a horizontal row, next the king, the queen, knave, ten,

nine, eight, seven, and six, as they appear from the pack. On these you form
the families, of thirteen cards each, piling downwards, not following suit, and
ending each family with the number
next to the bottom card, so that you,
will finish, if successful, with a row of
piles whose top cards number from the
ace to the seven, inclusive. Put the
cards that you cannot immediately use
in a stock. You can take up this stock,
re-shuffle it, and re-lay it twice.

You must be very careful to observe
when your families are complete, for as
each one ends with a different number,
you will be likely to put on too many
cards if you are inattentive.

FOURTEEN.

TWO PACKS.

THIS pretty little game is very simple, and requires little or no skill.
Lay off five rows of five cards each.
Look over the rows both perpendicu-
larly and horizontally. If in any row,
either way, you find two cards whose
pits number fourteen, you can throw
them out, and fill their places with others from the pack. Fill the spaces in
the same order in which you first laid
out the cards.

The knave counts as eleven, the
queen twelve, the king thirteen. If
your places are all full, and you can
take none out before the pack is ex-

hausted, you have the privilege of ex-
changing the place of two cards. Should
you still have no vacant places, you
have failed in the game. When the
pack is exhausted, take the cards in the
lower rows. Shuffle them, and fill up
the empty places in the other rows.
Continue to do this till you have used
up all the cards, when you will have
succeeded in mastering the game of
fourteen.

THE WINDMILL.

TWO PACKS.

THIS is one of those pretty games which forms a pleasing figure during the process of filling up the families. You can exercise your ingenuity in so placing the cards as to make the resemblance to the sails of a windmill as complete as possible.

Select an ace, and place it in the centre. Then, from your well-shuffled pack, take the first eight cards, and place them around it in a circle, leaving a free space between. When the first four kings appear, place one above,

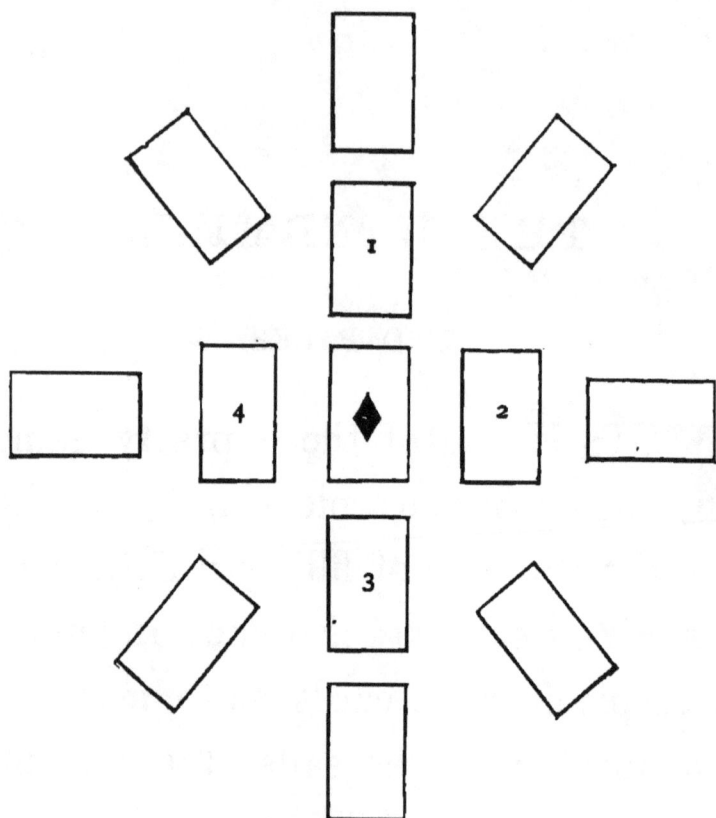

THE WINDMILL.
1, 2, 3, 4, THE KINGS' PLACES.

one below, and one on each side of the central ace. We have added a diagram to make this perfectly clear. You form your families downward on these kings, and upward on the ace in the centre, not following suit. You can use the cards in the sails of the mill, and replace them either from the stock or the pack. You put all the cards which you do not immediately use in the stock. When the family in the centre is completed, you put another ace on the king, and proceed in the same manner, until you have all the four aces, with their complete families, in the centre pile.

S A L I Q U E   L A W.

TWO PACKS.

THIS is one of the most interesting and pretty of these games. It takes its name from the famous law of feudal times, by which the female descendants of the royal families were excluded from all share in the government.

Take two entire packs of cards and shuffle them well together. Then select any king from them, and lay it upon the table before you. Place the cards which you cannot at once use on this; or, in technical language, form a stock upon it. You place the cards in three rows. In the lower row you put the aces and all cards which will follow in regular succession up to the knave, without regard to the suit. The queens are placed in the middle row, and the kings, with the stock upon them, in the upper row. When you meet another king, you place the first one in the upper row, with the stock upon it, and make a stock on the second, going on thus till the pack is exhausted. You can use the top card from these piles whenever opportunity offers. When the pack is out, if you have any kings uncovered, you can take the top cards from other piles and place on them, thus freeing the card beneath. Should you not in this way be enabled to complete your rows, you have finally the privilege of drawing one card from the upper piles, and placing it upon the lower. If you succeed, you will have all the court cards on the table in three rows, the kings at the head; the queens, who have performed their feudal duty of looking pretty and doing nothing, in the second row; and the knaves, with the common cards beneath them, in the third. There is much skill in selecting the cards judiciously from the top piles, as you are allowed to look at the under ones in this game.

PUSH PIN.

TWO PACKS.

THIS is a favorite game, and is very entertaining. It requires quick observation, but no other skill. You must allow plenty of room for it on your table. Lay out the cards in a straight line. If any card is between two of the same suit, or two of the same value, you push it out of the line, letting the others close up to fill its place. Removing one card will often ·bring others into the position which enables you to push them out. Also, if you have several cards of the same suit be-

tween any two of the same number, you
may throw them all out. When you
have laid out all the cards, you may remove the first card to the end of the
row, which may make new combinations
possible. The game succeeds if you
can push out all the cards but two.

LITTLE LOTS.

EUCHRE PACK.

WE have, in this funny little game, again a new variety. You use only what is called a Euchre pack, that is, a pack of the thirty-two highest cards only, counting the ace the highest, and so downward, with the court cards, to the sevens.

Lay off the cards in eight lots of four cards each, turning the top card face uppermost. Then take off all the couples of the top cards which match, and lay them aside. You may then turn up the top cards of those piles from which

4

you have removed a card, and form your couples anew, until you no longer have any two cards that will match. Should you succeed, you will of course have matched all the cards, and leave none upon the table. You have one privilege. If you have any piles containing only two cards left, you may turn up both cards, and if they match each other, you may remove them from the table, and so win the game.

The game is entirely one of chance, requiring no skill. It is, however, a favorite in Switzerland, and is sometimes used as a means of foretelling the good or ill luck of the player in some trifling affair.

WANDERING CARD.

ONE PACK.

THIS interesting game is on an entirely new principle, the object not being to form families, but a regular succession of piles of cards, from ace to king, each pile containing four cards of the same number.

Lay thirteen cards down in a row, with their faces upward. Then begin and lay down another layer of cards on the top of these, counting the number of the place as you do so. The knaves count eleven, the queens twelve, the kings thirteen. If the number of pits

on the card corresponds to the number
of the place on which it is laid, you put
it aside and go on. You repeat this
until you have four on each pile, except
in those cases where you have laid one
aside.

Take the top card from those laid
aside, and put it under the pile of the
corresponding number. Take the top
card from that pile, and put it also under the pile to whose number it corresponds. Continue to do this with the
top card of the pile, under which you
put another, until you come to one
which is already in its right place.
Then take another of the cards which
you have laid aside. Repeat this process as long as you have a card to use.
If successful. you will have a regular

succession of piles, from ace to king. You will often be amused to find that you have succeeded just as you thought yourself about to fail.

PATIENCE AT ST. HELENA.

TWO PACKS.

THIS game is said to have been in-
vented at St. Helena, and played
there by Napoleon Bonaparte. No-
where could patience have been more
needed. It must have been an impres-
sive sight to see this mighty emperor,
who had made and unmade kings by
his word, beguiling the hours of cap-
tivity with this quiet game of cards.
The game is unusually complicated,
and might well tax even his mental
powers to achieve success.

Place four kings, of different suits, in

one horizontal row. Place underneath them the four corresponding aces. The object of the game is to form the families upon these, descending from the kings, and ascending from the aces. You must follow suit. Having your two packs well shuffled together, you lay off a row underneath the aces, another row above the kings; place one card at the right end of each row of kings and aces, and one also at the left end. You must always observe this same order in laying off the cards. During the first distribution of the pack, you can only use the cards above the kings to put on the kings, and those below the aces to put on the aces; but you may use the side cards for either row. You have also the privilege of making mar-

riages, and in the judicious use of this
privilege lies the great skill of the game.
By marriage, we mean the placing of
one card on the top of another, which is
either just above or just below it in
rank. This often enables you to free
the card beneath, which you want, and
to have a sequence of cards ready for
use when opportunity offers. Besides
this, in this game marriage may enable
you to put a card in the side lines,
when you can use it for either row.
But you must also be very careful to
consider whether you are likely to want
the cards in the upward or downward
families, as it depends upon this circumstance whether you will cover with the
higher card or the lower. You repeat
these rows until the pack is used up.

It is considered the height of skill to complete your families during this first distribution, and Napoleon may have felt a momentary pleasure when he did so, as if he had gained a hard-fought battle. If you are not successful in this, however, you may take up the piles, and shuffle them, and lay them twice over; and in this case you can use the upper cards in the rows, indiscriminately, to put on the kings or the aces.

NUMBER ELEVEN.

ONE OR TWO PACKS.

PLACE six cards in one row, and five in the row underneath.

The aim is to form the number eleven with two cards. Any card which will form this number can be taken out, and their places filled from the pack. If a king, queen, and knave. are in one row, or are all of one suit, they count eleven, and can be removed at once. If the cards can be all used before the rows are complete, the game succeeds.

This is a very simple game, and very suitable for children, as it teaches them to see the relation of numbers, and add them quickly.

THE EGYPTIAN.

ONE PACK.

THIS game, named in honor of a distinguished gentleman representing our country in Egypt, is, as its name would indicate, one of the most interesting and most difficult of these games of Patience. It gives an opportunity for the exercise of great skill and foresight in making the combinations of which it admits. You will require ample space for it, as all the cards are laid upon the table at once.

In the middle of the table place the four aces in a row, one above the other.

Then begin at the left hand and lay off the cards as they come from the pack, placing five on the left side of the ace, beginning at the outside, and five at the right hand of the ace, leaving off at the outside. Do the same with the other aces, when you will have eight cards remaining. These you will place in a lower line, leaving an open space in the middle, under the aces. You must always observe this same order in laying out the cards.

Your object will now be to form the families on the aces in the centre, following suit. For this purpose, you can use only the end cards of each row. This would give you very limited means, had you not the privilege of marriages, i. e., of placing any end card on any other end card of the same suit that is one number higher or lower. This enables you often to remove a card from the end, and so free one next to it which you wish to use. If, by this means, you are able to free an entire row of cards, you then have a great opportunity, for you can then take any end card you please and put it next to the centre, and it becomes an end card, on which you can form a marriage, or which you may use at pleasure. If, after laying out the cards, you find no end cards that you can use, and none that you can move to form marriages you cannot go a step farther; you must take up the cards and try again. But if you once get a line freed, by planning out your game well, you will almost always succeed, and having once got well started, every step becomes easier. Some authorities allow the privilege of drawing a card from the rows which can be placed either on the centre piles or in marriage on the outer cards.

Companionship is very agreeable in this game, as one person often sees the possibility of new combinations which have escaped another. ·You need never despair as long as you can see anything new to be done, for it is surprising how the change of one card will open up new possibilities. This game well illustrates the motto, *"C'est le premier pas qui coûte."*

5

THE CLOCK.

ONE PACK.

THE principle of this game is the same as that of the Wandering Card, but it is modified so as to make a very pretty figure. It is, besides, a little more difficult to succeed in it.

Take off the cards in piles of four, and place them, face downward, in a circle on the table, so as to represent the dial of a clock. Put the thirteenth pile in the centre. You then number the places as in a clock, beginning at one and going round to eleven, to be represented by the knave, and

THE CLOCK.

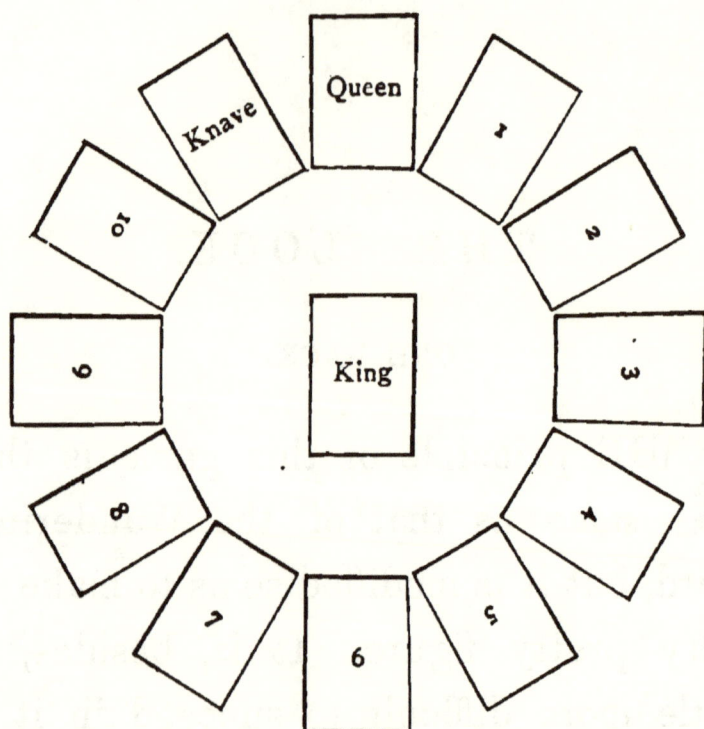

twelve by the queen. Now, take the top card from the centre pile, and put it under the pile of the corresponding number, with its face upwards, taking off the top card and putting it under the pile whose number corresponds to it. Continue to do this until you come to a king, which you put under the centre pile, taking another card from the top of that to renew your work. If successful, you will have thirteen piles of four cards each, face upwards, making a very pretty dial of a clock.

To make this perfectly clear, we have added a diagram of the arrangement of the cards.

DOUBLE JUMP.

ONE PACK.

THIS is a bright little game, which requires you to have your eyes open all the time. It resembles Push Pin, but is differently played.

Lay the cards out singly on the table, in a row. As you lay them down, if you find two of the same suit or number, with two cards between them, you place them on each other, and push up your cards to fill up the space. Every move may make a new arrangement, which will enable you to repeat this. When you can jump over no more, you lay down again from the pack, until you have a new opportunity for a jump. Remember that you must always pass over two. If you can thus reduce the number of your piles to three, you may then jump over one on to the same suit or number; and when you have two piles, you may put them together, if they agree in suit or number. Always jump forwards, that is, from left to right.

We should hardly call it failure, if you reduce your piles to the number of four; but if you can bring them all into one, it will be a brilliant success.

NIVERNAISE.

TWO PACKS.

THIS is one of the most difficult of these games, and you may try many times before you succeed in it, when your pleasure in success will be proportionally great. Having shuffled your two packs well together, place four cards on your right and four on your left, in perpendicular lines. Between these place six piles, of four cards each, from the pack, in a horizontal line, beginning at the left hand. From the top of these piles, or from the side cards, you take the kings and aces as they appear, and place them in two horizontal rows below the piles. The vacancies left in the side rows may be filled either from the top of the piles or from the pack. You form your families downward upon the kings, and upward upon the aces, following suit. When you can no longer find any cards of the right number to place in your families, either in the side rows or on the top of your piles, you place four more cards on each pile, and use the top cards again. You go on thus till the whole pack is exhausted, always dealing four cards at a time. You may take up the piles and shuffle them, and lay them down again, twice over. But even with this liberty, you may try many times before you will succeed in forming your families completely.

DUCHESS OF LUYNES.

TWO PACKS.

THIS curious game requires constant attention, or you will make
mistakes in placing your cards. Having shuffled your two packs well together, lay off the first four cards, call-
ing their places one, two, three, and
four. You put the fifth and sixth cards
in a stock. When the aces and kings
appear, you place them, following suit,
in two horizontal lines, the kings above
and the aces below, and form the families upon them, piling from the kings
down to aces, and from the aces upward

to kings. You can use the top cards either from the piles or from the stock. Go on laying off your piles in the same order, not filling up the place with another card, if you use one for the families, and always putting the fifth and sixth cards in the stock and rows. You can renew the stock twice. You have also the privilege of taking up the rows and stock once more, and laying the cards down in the row of four, but without the stock of the fifth and sixth cards. Should you not succeed in completing your families, then you will have failed, and must give your patience a new trial.

PICTURE.

TWO PACKS.

PLACE nine cards in three rows, called the Picture. Put the four kings in a vertical line, on the left of the picture, and the four aces in the same manner on the right. On these you will form the families, by piling upward from the aces to the kings, and downward from the kings to the aces, following suit. You can use any card from the picture that will take its place in the families. The cards which cannot immediately be used in the families are put in a stock, and you may fill up the vacant places in the picture either from the stock or the pack. You may turn the stock twice, playing from the pack and picture in the same manner as before.

If successful, your picture will prove a dissolving view and disappear.

LADY OF THE MANOR.

TWO PACKS.

THIS is not a very difficult game,
but it is one of the prettiest and
most interesting, and is quite unlike
any other. Having shuffled your packs
well together, lay off four piles of
twelve cards each, and place them in
a horizontal row with the faces up.
Then lay off the rest of the cards
in thirteen piles, forming a semicircle
around this row. Each pile should contain only cards of the same number, and
they should be placed in regular order.

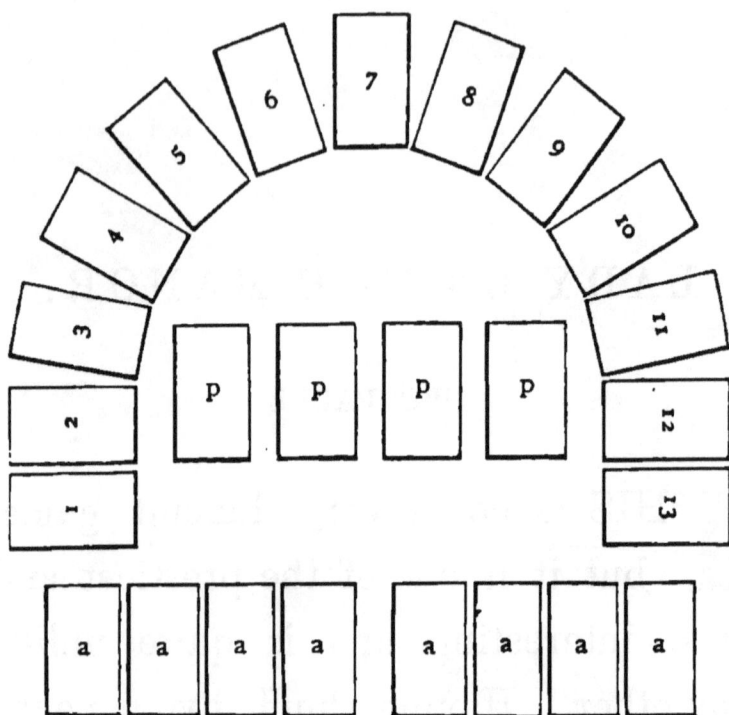

the aces being on the left and the kings on the right. You may then begin to form your families, by placing the aces in a horizontal row, at the base of the semicircle. On these you put the other cards in succession, without being obliged to follow suit. You can use the top cards of the piles of twelve which you first formed or any card in the semicircle. There is a very pleasant opportunity to show your skill in deciding when to have recourse to the semicircle for a card, as it is always more advantageous to use from the piles when possible. The only danger of failure will come from exhausting the piles in the semicircle before you have completed your families.

The Lady of the Manor seldom fails, however, to entertain her friends both agreeably and successfully.

HONORS.

TWO PACKS.

THIS game is less pleasing than many others, and requires close attention; still, as it is curious and somewhat different from any other, we give it a place.

Having shuffled the two packs together, you place in the upper row the deuce of spades, king of hearts, ace of diamonds, and queen of clubs; in the lower row, king of spades, queen of hearts, knave of diamonds, and ten of clubs. The families in the upper row are to be piled upward, that is, from ace to king, until the suit is complete; but in the lower row, they are to be piled downward, towards the ace; but each family must end with the card next in rank to that with which it began.

You now lay off two rows of cards of ten each. When these are full, you may lay another card upon each, choosing the place on which to put it according to your pleasure. Of course you will take care to leave those cards uncovered which you are likely soon to need. It is also well to put two cards of the same suit and number together. When your places are all filled, you may lay off three cards from the pack, and even draw one of those from the table. Still more, when the pack is out, if you' have any empty spaces in the rows, you may fill them with the top card of the double piles, thus freeing the card beneath. With all these privileges you ought to succeed, when you will have the aces of spades, two kings and queens of hearts, and kings and queens of diamonds, and the knaves of clubs on the top of the piles. You will see that the hearts and diamonds are' united in pairs of kings and queens, while the aces and knaves represent the estate of single blessedness.

PUZZLE.

EUCHRE PACK.

THIS little game is rather of the nature of Everlasting, but it is very simple; at least it is easy to begin it, but not so easy to finish it. It is not the first step that costs here, but the last.

Lay four cards in a row. If a king occurs, place it in a row above, and fill up the place. Continue laying the other cards on these four piles, placing the kings, as they come, in a row above. You must then fill up the families in the descending series, using only the

top card of the pile immediately below.
When you find no top card that you can
use, take up the piles and re-lay them,
and again use only the top card to
fill up your families. If the series is
complete before your patience is exhausted, you have won the game.

KNAVES' DIAL.

ONE OR TWO PACKS.

THIS is the first game which makes any distinction of color, yet it is careful to put both black and red on an equality. You may begin with whichever you prefer. The object is to form a dial with the figures, and the cards are placed as in the diagram of the Clock.

Deal a card from the pack, and put it in its appropriate place in the dial, according to its number; the queens will represent eleven and the kings twelve.

Put the knave, when it comes, in the centre.

You now play from the pack, putting cards of the same suit as the first one in their respective places in the dial. The cards which you cannot use are to be put into a stock. Having completed this first dial, you then put the other cards on their numbers, with this restriction, that the colors must alternate. If your first suit was black, you must now put on red, and the reverse. You may turn your stock twice, and you will probably succeed in making a very pretty dial of a color different from that with which you began.

BRUNETTE AND BLONDE.

TWO PACKS.

PLACE eight cards in one row. Place the aces, as they come, in a row above. On these eight cards you may place any which you lay off from the pack, which are next to them in the descending line, if the color is reversed. That is, you can put a red eight on a black nine, or a black nine on a red ten, and so on.

As soon as any cards, either in the stock or among the eight cards, can be put, in their order, upon the aces, you may place them there; but it must be again with alternating colors. On a red ace you must put a black deuce, on a red three a black four, and so on. When any vacancies are left in the line, they may be filled either from the stock or pack.

You may turn the stock twice. If successful, the Blonde and Brunette will share in the Victory equally.

THE SQUARE.

TWO PACKS.

THIS is a very simple game, requiring no skill, but attention to putting on the cards as soon as opportunity offers.

Place four cards before you, and four
in a line on the right and four on the
left, so as to form three sides of a square.
Place the eight aces, as they turn up,
in two rows within the square. Place
on the twelve cards of the square all
those of the same suit in the descending line, and on the aces those in the
ascending line. You can use the top

card from the square, or from the pack, to complete your families on the aces. Those cards that cannot be placed in either form a stock. Whenever you can place one card upon another, in the descending line, in the square, you can do so, filling the vacancy from the stock or pack.

No second distribution is allowed, as the first gives you a fair chance of success.

THE QUEEN'S PARTY.

ONE PACK.

LAY off four rows of four cards each, making a hollow square, with space for eight cards in a circle inside. This is called the ante-chamber. In this all the guests must wait until their appropriate time for entering the audience hall. The audience hall is the space inside the ante-chamber. The kings and queens must come in together, and take their places thus: The king and queen of hearts at the top, of diamonds at the bottom, of clubs at the right, and of spades at the left, the queens being on top of the kings. The aces or emperors must be accompanied by the knaves, and take their places between the queens. On the knaves, the common people, or lower cards, will take their places, according to suits, downward to the deuces.

You will take from the ante-chamber any king and queen, or ace and knave, of the same suit, and put them in their respective places, and fill the spaces in the antechamber from the stock or pack. Lay off the cards from the pack, putting any which you cannot immediately place either in the audience-room or ante-chamber, in a stock. You cannot turn the stock, but can only fill vacancies in the ante-chamber. Of course, if you succeed, your ante-chamber will be empty, and your suits complete.

FIFTEEN IN A ROW.

TWO PACKS.

THIS game resembles the Egyptian, but is somewhat differently arranged, and is played with two packs, instead of one.

Lay out all the cards of both packs in rows of fifteen each, except the last row, which will contain only fourteen. Let each row lie half way upon the one above it. When all the cards are spread out, take the aces and kings from the last row. Place these as best suits your convenience for forming on them the families. On the aces you will

form upward, on the kings downward.
If there are no aces or kings in the last
row, see whether, by marriages, you
can uncover the kings or aces in the
sixth row. If you cannot, you may
take them from the sixth row, and fill
the spaces left by them with the cards
immediately below them. After you
have one ace and one king, you can use
all the cards which are independent,
that is, which have no other leaning
upon them, and can either make marriages with them, or give them their
places in the families. You must follow
suit, both in making marriages and in
placing cards in the families. Whenever you have a line free from top to
bottom, it is called a street. In this
street you may place any independent

card, and add to it any that follow either in ascending or descending series. This gives you a fresh opportunity for new combinations, and if you can once obtain a street, you may confidently hope to win this difficult game. Success is of course achieved by completing your families.

NAPOLEON, OR THE PET GAME.

TWO PACKS.

LAY off four rows of ten cards each, the lower row lapping over the upper. You can use only the cards in the lower row, but when any card in that row is taken away, the one above it becomes the lowest or free card, and can be used. You can also make marriages by putting any card on the one next higher of the same suit, if both are free. After the cards are laid out the aces are placed in a line below, and the families are formed on them by piling regularly upwards by suits.

When you can use a card in the upper row, and so leave a clear space, you can fill this space with the top card, either of the stock or pack, but you cannot fill spaces in any but the top row, or put any card already on the table in the upper row. Place all cards which you cannot immediately use on the aces in a stock, and use the top card whenever you have opportunity. You can turn the stock twice.

THE PET GAME.

A variation of this game has received the name of Pet, from its popularity in a large family. In this game, you place the cards as before, but you can make marriages from the stock or pack, by placing the top card on the one next above it, and you can also place any free card on an empty space in the first row. This gives you great opportunity of re-arranging the cards already on the table, but to make up for it, there is no privilege of turning the stock.

THE OLD STAGER.

TWO PACKS.

L AY off three rows of thirteen cards each. If in doing so you place a king on a lower number of the same suit, you have the privilege of removing it to the next place, filling up this space with the next card from the pack, as it would be almost impossible to succeed with a king thus placed.

After the cards are laid out, place the aces as they come in a row below, and pile on them by suits from ace to king. You can use only the lowest row of cards, but when the lower card is removed, the one next above it becomes free for use. You can also form marriages by placing a free card on another free card of the denomination just above it of the same suit. You can also place the top card from the stock or pack either on the aces in order, or on the rows. When you have a space in the upper row, you can fill it only with the top card of the stock; but you can place another free card upon that one if it is next below it in number. If you do not succeed, you have the privilege of laying off three cards from the under side of the stock, and then going on as before.

CORNERS.

ONE PACK.

THIS is a very convenient game, because it takes only one pack and very little space, but it requires very close attention.

The cards are placed as hereafter directed, in three rows of three each, thus forming a nearly square figure, and the families when completed will occupy the corners. After shuffling your pack, lay the top card in the left hand top corner. Whatever its denomination, it forms the basis of the pile on which the cards must be placed upwards in order, following suit until the family is complete.

Thus, if the first card be a nine, the cards must be ranged thus: 9, 10, knave, queen, king, 1, 2, 3, 4, 5, 6, 7, 8, ending with eight. When the same numbers of the other suits appear, they must be placed on the other corners, and the families formed on them in the same manner. Place the next top cards of the pack on the other spaces in the square. When these places are all full, reserving the corners for the regular families, you must form a stock of all cards which you cannot immediately use. But you can at any time form marriages by placing a lower card on a higher, either from the top of the stock or pack, or from one of the centre piles on to another, if a vacant space can be thus made; in the centre piles you can fill it either from the stock or pack.

Remember that in the corners the cards are always to be piled upwards, that is, a higher on a lower card, following suit, while in the other spaces you place a lower card on a higher, and are not obliged to follow suit, although it is always for your interest to do so when you can. When the cards are played out, if your game is successful, the four suits will be regularly piled in the four corners, and the intervening spaces left empty.

You may be in danger of forgetting the number of the card which was first played, and so neglecting to place the corresponding numbers of other suits

on the corners, and also of getting con-
fused in regard to piling up and down
in different places.

Do not forget that an ace goes on a
king in the corners, but on a deuce in
the other places. There is much skill
in using the privilege of marriage to
the best advantage.

RANK AND FILE.

TWO PACKS.

LAY off eleven cards in a row across the table.

Take a king and an ace of each suit from this row if you can find them there, with which to begin your families, piling upwards on the aces and downwards on the kings, following suit.

You can use any card in this row which comes in order upon them. Fill the spaces in this row from the pack. When it is full, lay out the next row,

slightly lapping upon it. Of this row
you can use only the two right hand
end cards. Continue laying out the
cards in rows, using the two end cards
as you have a chance, until the pack is
exhausted. You may then use the
lower row of cards, or any one left uncovered, by using that below it. You
can also form marriages either upwards
or downwards with any free cards. If
you clear a line upwards completely,
you can place any free king in the
vacant space, but no other card. This
will relieve some card above it.

If you are unsuccessful in completing
the families by the first laying out, you
must begin at the left hand lower
corner and take up the cards by lines
into a pack, without shuffling; you relay

them under the same conditions as
before.

You can thus relay the cards twice,
which gives you a fair chance for success.

THE TOAD.

TWO PACKS.

D O not be frightened at the name of this game, which is a very harmless one. It is simple and easy, if not as interesting as many others.

Place in a pile thirteen cards, as they come from the pack. This pile is called the Toad. Lay off the other cards in five piles, which you may arrange as you please. When the aces appear, you may lay them in a horizontal line below. You will form the families upon these without following suit. You can use the top cards of the piles and the top card of the toad in forming the families. If you succeed, of course the toad will disappear, and all the cards will find their appropriate places in families.

The toad always stands ready to come in with his help. This is a favorite game with some old players of Patience.

EXPLANATION

———•◦•———

Pack. The whole series of fifty-two cards, or in Patience often a double series of two packs in one, or one hundred and four cards, is called The Pack. This is held in the hand to play from, and whatever remains in the hand is still called the Pack.

Piquet or Euchre Pack. In Piquet or Euchre only the thirty-two highest cards —including the ace and the court cards down to the seven —are used; hence a pack of these thirty-two cards is called a Euchre or Piquet Pack.

Suits. Cards of the same kind, as hearts, spades, diamonds, clubs, without reference to the number of spots.

Pips. The spots on the cards; that is, the figures of clubs, diamonds, &c.

Court Cards, originally *Coat Cards*, are the picture
cards. These, being dressed in costume, were called
Coat Cards. They are the King, Queen, and Knave.

Honors. The aces, together with the court cards, are
called the *Honors.*

Families. The series of cards beginning with th. .ace
and ending with the king in regular succession, or
the reverse, beginning with the king and ending with
the ace. The series must be all of one suit only when
directed to follow suit.

Stock. The cards that cannot be immediately used as
they come from the pack, are often put in a pile on
the table together. These are called a *Stock.* To
turn Stock is to take them up, re-shuffle them or not,
as you please, and use them as you did the original
pack.

Marriage. The union of one card with another, just
above or just below it in rank, — as the queen with
the king or knave, the nine with the eight or ten, &c.
Sometimes the word is specially applied to the union
of kings and queens.

www.ingramcontent.com/pod-product-compliance
Lightning Source LLC
Chambersburg PA
CBHW030537270326
41927CB00008B/1413